Praying With
Saint Paul

SAINT SHENOUDA PRESS

Praying With
Saint Paul

by: Viola Yassa

ST SHENOUDA PRESS
SYDNEY, AUSTRALIA
2017

Praying with Saint Paul

ST SHENOUDA PRESS
8419 Putty Rd,
Putty, NSW, 2330
Australia

www.stshenoudapress.com

ISBN 13: 978-0-9945710-7-6

CONTENTS

CONTENTS

PRAYER OF FAITH

Saul appears not to have known much, if anything, about Christ: yet he 'breathed threats and murder' against the unknown, through persecuting Christ's followers. Today, atheists, and others, who claim not to believe in God, spend a surprising amount of time and energy in speaking against that which (so they say) is not merely unknown; but does not actually exist. Saul was no atheist. He had devoted his life to achieving the highest levels within the Hebrew religion: he spent a surprising amount of time and energy in speaking and acting against Christianity, which, so it seems, he believed had no right to exist.

Saul was strong. Saul was powerful. Saul was Zealous and fuelled by the feverish fear that his name could inspire. Saul was a big shot on an important big shot business trip, carrying celebrity endorsements from the mega priests of his day. In an age where word-of-mouth didn't mean five-thousand Facebook friends fanning the flame, but literally "word-of-mouth," Saul was a well-known brand tied to terror and synonymous with steely strength. Saul was simply... "In Control"

"As he journeyed he came near Damascus, and suddenly a light shone around him from heaven. Then he fell to the ground, and heard a voice saying to him, "Saul, Saul, why are you persecuting Me?" And he said, "Who are You, Lord?" Then the Lord said, "I am Jesus, whom you are persecuting. It is hard for you to kick against the goads." Acts9:3-5.

When Saul cried out to God, in anguish "Who are You, Lord?" it must have been a big surprise, at the least when the answer was not given in Old Testament terms: saying: 'I am the God of Abraham, Isaac and Israel; and this is what I command of you'. Such an approach would, probably, have done no more than to confirm Saul's existing standpoints, and to justify, in his mind at least, his attempts to stamp out what he believed to be a heresy.

Instead, the answer was given in up-to-the-moment modern terms: "I Am Jesus". It went against Saul's previous experience, against his set way of life, and against his belief that Christianity was heretical: for the voice said: 'I am (present tense) Jesus, (Christ's earthly name) with the powerful implication of: 'Not dead: but very much alive'.

The first surprise, was followed by another: 'I am Jesus, whom you are persecuting: with the equally powerful implication, that hurt done to any of Christ's followers, was hurt done to Christ Himself. Jesus bypassed Saul's highly trained mind: and went straight to the depths of his humanity, at heart level, and got a positive response.

"Who are You, Lord?" The whole of Saul's life was reduced to these four words. The light pierced the darkness of his soul and with laser intensity burned away everything but the risen Christ. His pride, his previous purposes, his plans... all of it disintegrated in the shadow of the spoken acknowledgment of who was indeed Lord.

It took a bit of 'drama' to change Saul: He underwent radical, positive and life-altering change when he encountered the Lord. Through revelation, he discovered that he was not called to defend the Hebrew religion; but to become the dedicated servant of Jesus; and to promote the Christian faith, wherever the Lord sent him.

"And I thank Christ Jesus our Lord who has enabled me, because He counted me faithful, putting me into the ministry, although I was formerly a blasphemer, a persecutor, and an insolent man; but I obtained mercy because I did it ignorantly in unbelief. And the Grace of our Lord was exceedingly abundant, with faith and love which are in Christ Jesus. This is a faithful saying and worthy of all acceptance, that Christ Jesus came into the world to save sinners, of whom I am chief. However, for this reason I obtained mercy, that in me, first Jesus Christ might show all long-suffering, as a pattern to those who are going to believe on Him for everlasting life. Now to the King eternal, immortal, invisible, to God who alone is wise, be honour and glory forever and ever. Amen," (I Timothy 1:12-17)

When we were baptised our godparent (sponsor) was the one who renounced Satan and accepted Christ for us. They were the one who confessed the "I believe" of the Nicene Greed for us. But if we are to be true Christians, there must be a time in life when we must say these words for ourselves, a time when we ourselves decide for Christ and commit our whole being to Him as our personal Lord and Saviour. Unless this happens we are Christians in name only. Belief is something personal, something you must do for yourself, something nobody else can do for you. No one will ever get to heaven on someone else's faith. We need to believe in a contemporary Christ and take the leap of faith in our daily life.

What makes a Christian a Christian is this personal commitment to Christ. One's formal belonging to the Church through Baptism and other sacramental participation remains a mere potential if the individual commitment does not take place. The sacramental gifts of Baptism and Eucharist and of all the Sacraments are essential for an objective membership in the body of Christ; but again they are pure potentials if a conversion of the heart and mind does not occur at some point in life.

Faith is confidence in God that leads us to believe His Word, the Holy Bible. In Romans 10:9, St Paul explains that besides the knowledge and intellectual faith which involves our mind, we have to decide for or against Christ and His offer of salvation. This means that faith involves our will as well. "If you confess with your mouth and believe in your heart that God has raised the Lord Jesus from the dead, you will be saved".

To say "I believe in Christ" is to believe in Christ who lives today, not just an important historical figure. The kind of Christ I believe in, speaks to me today. He is present with me today. He judges me today. He is a contemporary Christ.

To say "I believe in Christ" is to know God in Christ. To know that He loves me, that He came down from heaven for me, that He gave His life for me. In view of all this, I can safely trust that no matter what He allows to come to me, there is meaning and purpose and love behind it: God's

The Holy Scriptures: Just as in paradise, God walks in the Holy Scriptures, seeking man
—St Ambrose

The Lord sought Saul and revealed Himself to him. He does the same with us in one form or another. After encountering the Lord, you become overwhelmed with His love. Jesus is your "first love". You couldn't stop thinking of

Him all the time. You talked to Him almost constantly. The Word of God was fascinating with the Holy Spirit opening up new revelations to you as you devoured the Word daily. These "good works" came automatically. They were the works of the Holy Spirit. It took no effort on your part; it was just a result of the encounter with God.

"He who has My commandments and keeps them, it is he who loves Me. And he who loves Me will be loved by My Father, and I will love him and manifest Myself to him" (John 14:21)

When Jesus is our "first love", we walk in the Spirit; all the works we did were by simply believing God. All works were by the power of the Spirit not the flesh. The results were amazing! It took no effort to succeed for it was God working it in you. God lifted us up, God cleansed us, God picked us up out of the pit because of His mercy, not for any good works we did. It was God the Holy Spirit who opened up the Scriptures to us and kept the Word fresh and gave us revelations. It was the Holy Spirit who led the relationship and kept it fresh and exciting. We simply followed Him keeping our eyes focused on Him.

In the beginning we didn't know enough to let pride take us down the wrong way. Our heart was soft and pliable toward God when He was our "first love". We were open to new truths in the Word and teachable knowing nothing and relied on God alone to lead us. You only believed. You had a faith in Jesus your "first love", knowing that He alone will cause you to stand before the Father sinless. Because of the Blood of Jesus alone you were justified. There was a leaning on Jesus, a trust in Him to work all things out in you and joy filled your heart. You knew you were justified by His blood and saved by His Grace.

Whereas your life was once filled with unbelief, the root and foundation of all sin, now you have utmost confidence and faith in God and His Word. There may have been a time when pride was at the very centre of your life. You had ambitious thoughts of yourself, powers, desires and aims; but now that will begin to change. There may have been a time when there was hatred in your life. Envy, discontent and malice filled your thoughts toward others. That too will gradually change.

"I know your works, your labour, your patience, and that you cannot bear those who are evil. And you have tested those who say they are apostles and are not, and have found them liars; and you have persevered and have patience, and have laboured for My name's sake and have not become weary. Nevertheless, I have this against you, that you have left your first love. Remember therefore from where you have fallen; repent and do the first works, or else I will come to you quickly and remove your lamp-stand from its place — unless you repent," (Revelations 2:2-5).

There was a time when you could easily tell a lie. There were falsehoods and hypocrisies in many of your thoughts, words and deeds. That is now all changed. There was a time when you gave in to the lust of the flesh. That is now changed. You may stumble into some of the traps that the devil puts out for you, but immediately you will be sorry, confess your sins and ask forgiveness. You live a life of repentance in which the new image of Christ is continually regenerated.

 Is there a longing in your heart for holiness; for sanctification; for purification; for Christ-likeness; for a greater conformity to the image of the Son of God? Confess to Him your sin and your need and He will satisfy the deepest longings of your heart. At what price? Part with sin and uncleanness for "by one offering, He has perfected forever those who are being sanctified," (Hebrews 10:14).

Faith brings me to the Lord Jesus, not only to obtain the forgiveness of sin, but also that I may enjoy the power which will make it possible for me, as a child of God, every moment. It also helps me to abide in Him, and to be numbered among His obedient children of whom it is written that, as He who has called them is holy, they also may be holy in all manner of conversation. We cannot possibly be satisfied with anything less than - each day, each hour, each moment, in Christ, through the power of the Holy Spirit - to walk with God.

Along with the deepest conviction that there is no good in you, confess that you see in the Lord Jesus all the goodness of which you have need, for the life of a child of God; and begin literally to live "by the faith of the Son of God, who loved me, and gave Himself for me," (Galatians 2.20). Just as, through faith, we found the fullness of forgiveness, so through a new act of faith, a real deliverance from the dominion of Sin which has so easily beset us is obtained, and the abiding blessing of the continuous experience of the keeping power of Christ becomes ours.

The love of Christ is the all-important thing for the child of God. The important thing is not: "Am I ever going to overcome my present struggles?" Nor is it our health. Nor is it that things go well in our families, so that there are no tragedies, no terrible sicknesses, and no sudden deaths. But the all-important question the child of God asks is, "Will anything separate me from the love of Jesus Christ?" The child of God will even say this: "I can bear to lose everything else in life! But I could never bear to lose the love of Christ! Never!"

"Who shall separate us from the love of Christ? Shall tribulation, or distress, or persecution, or famine, or nakedness, or peril, or sword? As it is written: "For Your sake we are killed all day long; we are accounted as sheep for the slaughter," (Romans 8:35-36). We need that love.

And we need to know that we have it

 Nothing shall separate the one who believes in truth from the ground of true faith. ... The man in union with truth knows clearly that all is well with him, even if everyone else thinks that he has gone out of his mind

— Pseudo-Dionysius

PRAYER OF OEBEDIENCE

"As he journeyed he came near Damascus, and suddenly a light shone around him from heaven. Then he fell to the ground, and heard a voice saying to him, "Saul, Saul, why are you persecuting Me?" And he said, "Who are You, Lord?" Then the Lord said, "I am Jesus, whom you are persecuting. It is hard for you to kick against the goads. So he, trembling and astonished, said, "Lord, what do You want me to do?" (Acts 9:3-6).

Have we ever felt the need to ask God: 'Who are you, Lord? And: 'What do you really require of me?' If so: did we respond to that need, and actually ask the question? Many Christians admit that: when given such opportunities; they failed to call upon God in that particular way: because they were afraid that they might receive a 'Damascus Road' type of reply? Today, there is a sense in which 'high and holy' talk about God, challenges the minds of some, but tends to pass most people by. It seems that, with us, too, appeals to the depths of our humanity, at heart level – produce our most positive and fulfilling responses.

What challenges the mind will, at best, remain theoretical, and abstract, until it is made concrete through 'hands-on' application and experience. What challenges the heart: opens us more directly to opportunities for experiencing God's activity; as He offers new aspects of spiritual life; a deeper faith, and a desire to be caught up in loving service and outreach. The impact of the challenge that came upon Saul, in his 'Damascus Road' experience; touches and influences us, today.

His formal training at Tarsus (one of the great universities of its day) together with him asking for, and receiving, letters from the authorities, made him 'official', and someone to be reckoned with. But Saul's question 'Who are you, Lord?' also proved that he had deeper needs: that his 'official standing' could not reach, let alone deal with.

What about us? We have 'standing' as citizens, taxpayers, employers, or employees, as Christians, with formal membership, as leaders, stewards, and in many other ways. But no matter how our 'standing' may be useful to us, and helpful to others: we remain people of spiritual needs, who; like Saul, in his need; must call out to the only one who can truly meet and fulfil them.

"Then the Lord said to him, "Arise and go into the city, and you will be told what you must do." And the men who journeyed with him stood speechless, hearing a voice but seeing no one. Then Saul arose from the ground, and when his eyes were opened he saw no one. But they led him by the hand and brought him into Damascus. (Acts 9:6-9).

St Paul's blindness may be taken as a symbol of 'none so blind as those who will not see'; and the restoration of his outward sight, as a symbol of a new, inner 'sight' being given, and received; that made him both willing and able to serve the Lord.

The men travelling with Saul: 'heard the sounds', but 'did not see anyone'. Today, as then, people can go about their 'religious' business; read the right books: listen to talks, sermons, hymns, prayers etc., and 'hear the sounds', without actually 'seeing' God, to whom the sounds are directed. They can share in a church service and, without having received a spiritual challenge; can walk out as unchanged as when they walked in.

All true faith is given: at first hand, by God. Therefore, we must ensure that we never risk preventing Christ imparting his: 'I am Jesus' love and care; at the time and place, and in the manner, that he chooses.

Largely, the Old Testament Jews believed that God confined his activities within the boundaries of 'The Promised Land'. Our New Testament text: began to change that; through revealing divine activity being undertaken beyond the borders of Israel - at Damascus, in Syria. Along with all Christians: we must be prayerfully alert against thinking that God always works within the boundaries of our understanding. For, such set-in-our-ways thinking; puts us at risk of not receiving new, life-changing, faith-deepening revelations.

God, who does not force things upon us: will not remove the boundaries that we create. Therefore, the Lord's gracious activity, going on beyond whatever limits that we may have set; cannot change and bless our lives, until we remove the said boundaries.

Saul's need; was far greater than his reluctance to ask for help. The received revelation made a new man of him; and, under his new name, St Paul: his example, and

teaching, became, and remains, of very great value to the Church; and to us, today.

"Now there was a certain disciple at Damascus named Ananias; and to him the Lord said in a vision, "Ananias."And he said, "Here I am, Lord.""

So the Lord said to him, "Arise and go to the street called Straight, and inquire at the house of Judas for one called Saul of Tarsus, for behold, he is praying. And in a vision he has seen a man named Ananias coming in and putting his hand on him, so that he might receive his sight."

Then Ananias answered, "Lord, I have heard from many about this man, how much harm he has done to Your saints in Jerusalem. And here he has authority from the chief priests to bind all who call on Your name."

But the Lord said to him, "Go, for he is a chosen vessel of Mine to bear My name before Gentiles, kings, and the children of Israel. For I will show him how many things he must suffer for My name's sake."

And Ananias went his way and entered the house; and laying his hands on him he said, "Brother Saul, the Lord Jesus, who appeared to you on the road as you came, has sent me that you may receive your sight and be filled with the Holy Spirit." Immediately there fell from his eyes something like scales, and he received his sight at once; and he arose and was baptised.

So when he had received food, he was strengthened. Then Saul spent some days with the disciples at Damascus," (Acts 9:10-19).

Ananias was afraid; and had established a mental barrier between himself and Saul. However, God's commands, overrode Ananias' reservations, enabling him to remove the barrier so much so, as to lay hands upon the needy Saul, and call him 'brother'. Not only that, for he went on to say: 'The Lord has sent me, so that you may see again, and be filled with the Holy Spirit'.

Can we say that we have never prevented the close

approach of someone who; as Ananias was, to Saul; may have been God-sent, to us, in order that 'we may see, and be filled with the Holy Spirit?' Can we be that sure?

What about our situations? Could it be that, somewhere along the line: reluctance on our part; to receive challenge; and to undergo change, created a barrier that has not yet been fully removed?

If we feel that there is still, something of a barrier, that stands in the way of our ongoing spiritual growth and development: would we dare to ask that very definite question of God, 'Who are you, Lord, and what is it that you require of me?'

 If we do ask; and the Lord replies: how prepared are we to gladly accept what the Lord offers: even if it is a 'Damascus Road' type of answer? Obey God and leave all the consequences to Him. If you will take this one principle to heart, you will have the awesome privilege of watching the Lord accomplish great things in and through you. There is nothing more important in life

than following Jesus Christ and trusting Him to take care of you.

"True perfection consists in having but one fear, the fear of losing God's friendship."
– St Gregory of Nyssa.

PRAYER OF SUBMISSION

"Who are you, Lord, and what is it that you require of me?" St Paul asked. The Lord's reply changed everything. Everything that gave Saul value, status, meaning, identity (oh, there's that word again) was stripped from him in a nanosecond.

Faith begins with receptivity. It begins when a man is at least willing to listen to the message of the truth. It goes on to mental assent. A man first hears and then agrees that this is true. But mental assent need not issue in action. Many a man knows very well that something is true, but does not change his actions to meet that knowledge. The final stage is when this mental assent becomes total surrender. In full-fledged faith, a man hears the Christian message, agrees that it is true, and then casts himself upon it in a life of total yielding.

"If anyone else thinks he may have confidence in the flesh, I more so: circumcised the eighth day, of the stock of Israel, of the tribe of Benjamin, a Hebrew of the Hebrews; concerning the law, a Pharisee; concerning zeal, persecuting the church; concerning the righteousness which is in the Law, blameless.

But what things were gain to me, these I have counted loss for Christ. Yet indeed I also count all things loss for the excellence of the knowledge of Christ Jesus my Lord, for whom I have suffered the loss of all things, and count them as rubbish, that I may gain Christ and be found in Him, not having my own righteousness, which is from the Law, but that which is through faith in Christ, the righteousness which is from God by faith; that I may know Him and the power of His resurrection, and the fellowship of His sufferings, being conformed to His death, if, by any means, I may attain to the resurrection from the dead," (Philippians 3:4-11).

After his encounter with Christ on the road to Damascus (Acts 9:1-9), St Paul then understood that his Jewish heritage and achievements neither qualified him for covenant membership nor marked him out as a member. Now, he considers those advantages and every other potential advantage to be a loss. Again, such consideration is, literally, "for the sake of" Christ.

What he formerly considered or would otherwise consider "gain" he now considers loss and even rubbish in order that he may "gain" intimacy with Christ. Does that mean that St Paul is looking forward to gaining Christ in the future? In a sense, yes. It's clear from Philippians 3:7 that he has already gained Christ, that he already knows Him personally and intimately, but it is also clear, as the passage unfolds, that there is more to gain, particularly and finally at "the resurrection from the dead."

What is it about Christ that causes this radical shift in values for St Paul and continues to govern his choices? He says it is the "surpassing greatness of knowing Christ Jesus my Lord." It's not that there is no value in anything else; it's just that the value of knowing Christ is greater – so much greater that St Paul can chalk up everything that would compete with "knowing Christ" as something that can be released.

What does it mean to know Christ? For St Paul, it is an intimate personal relationship with Christ. The word "know" is used in both the Hebrew Scriptures and the New Testament of sexual relations (Genesis 4:1, Matthew 1:25). Both testaments compare the Lord's covenant relationship with his people to marriage (Hosea 1-3,

Ephesians 5:25-27, Revelations 19:7-8). God is romancing us. The closest human parallel is the physical, emotional and spiritual intimacy experienced in sexual intercourse between a husband and a wife, but even that pales in comparison to the surpassing greatness of knowing Christ. For the sake of Christ, particularly knowing Christ, St Paul not only considers everything to be loss; he actually has lost all things.

Your first encounter with Christ may not be as dramatic as St Paul's, but after you meet Jesus, it will dawn on you that that your values will have to change. Whatever our culture puts forth as its identity markers will have to be re-evaluated in light of Christ. We all have a road to Damascus, though undoubtedly, not all of the high drama, 1st Century type. But there will be a moment or collection of moments when we are given the option to ask, "Who are you Lord? And on the basis of this, how should I live?" The answer is "For you have died, and your life is now hidden with Christ in God," (Colossians 3:3). My identity is buried in Christ. Know Him and I will know myself as the image of Him that He designed me to be. May God be glorified for everything that I am or hope to be. Amen.

In the Old Testament, Job prayed with submission

when he said, "Though He slay me, I will hope in Him," (Job 13:15). But it was Jesus that expressed the prayer of submission best. "Father, if You are willing, remove this cup from Me; yet not My will, but Yours be done," (Luke 22:42).

Jesus' prayer in the Garden of Gethsemane is a pattern for us. Christ could have avoided the cross. He did not have to go to Jerusalem that last time. He could have compromised with the priests, bargained with Caiaphas. Pilate wanted to release Him, all but begged Him to say the right words so that he might. In the Garden, Christ had plenty of time to flee, but He used His free will to leave the decision up to His Father.

Even when Christ was bowing to the possibility of death by crucifixion, He never forgot either the presence or the power of God. The prayer of submission must not be interpreted negatively. It does not let us lie down in the dust of a godless universe and steel ourselves just for the worst.

Rather it says, "This is my situation at the moment. I'll face the reality of it. But I'll also accept willingly whatever a loving Father sends." Acceptance, therefore, never slams the door on hope.

Yet even with hope our submission must be the real thing, because this giving up of self-will is the hardest thing we human beings are ever called on to do. It's good to remember that not even the Master Shepherd can lead if the sheep have not this trust in Him. That's the reason of Christ's insistence on practical obedience: "But why do you call Me, Lord, Lord, and not do the things which I say?" (Luke 6:46).

Our flexibility and submission must be complete, from our wills right on through to our actions. When we come right down to it, how can we make obedience real, except as we give over our self-will in reference to each of life's episodes as it unfolds? That's why it shouldn't surprise us that at the heart of the secret of answered prayer lies true submission.

"Return to Me and I will return to you says the Lord of hosts," (Malachi 3:7). When Christ enters into the human heart, He expects to be Lord and Master. He demands complete surrender. He demands control of your intellectual processes. He requires that your body be subject to Him. He expects you to surrender your talents and abilities to Him. He expects nothing less than that all your work and labour will be performed in His name. "Love the Lord your God with all your heart, all your mind and all your soul, and all your strength."

> "Prayer preserves temperance, suppresses anger, restrains pride and envy, draws down the Holy Spirit into the soul and raises man to heaven."
>
> — St Ephraim the Syrian

We point our fingers at the heathen and at the idol worshippers of old, but we are not different. We have come to worship things, status, fame, popularity, money, security. Anything that comes between God and our self is idolatry. Jesus demands Lordship over all such things. He wants you to yield everything concerning your social life, your family life, your business life to Him. He must have first place in everything you do or think or say, for when you truly repent you turn toward God in everything. Don't say, "I'll give up some of my sins and hang on to some others. I'll leave part of my life for Jesus and part for my own desires". Jesus expects 100% surrender.

When you have determined that you are renouncing sin, forsaking sin, and yielding all to Christ you have taken another step toward peace with God. "If we confess our sins, He is faithful and just to forgive us our sins and to cleanse us from all unrighteousness," (1 John 1:9).

"This is the great work of man; always to take the blame of his own sins before God and to expect temptations to his last breath."

— St Anthony the Great

"I surrender all. All to thee my precious Saviour, I surrender all". In these lines of an old hymn, we have the essence of the prayer of submission. One aspect of surrender to Holy Spirit is a loosening of our hold on certain things. Relinquish our own will in the matter and trust God for a bigger plan and purpose than we can see now. This means we attach less significance and importance to anything and everything. External goals become less and less important and an inner focus on the Heart becomes more and more primary; it becomes our primary source of happiness, of joy, of Grace and Ease.

The real secret of an unsatisfied life lies too often in an un-surrendered will. Surrender your own poverty and acknowledge your nothingness to the Lord. Whether you understand it or not, God loves you, is present in you, lives in you, dwells in you, calls you, saves you and offers you an understanding and compassion. There are different levels of surrender, all of which affect our relationship with God. Initial surrender to the drawing of the Holy Spirit leads to salvation (John 6:44; Acts 2:21). When we let go of our own attempts to earn God's favour and rely upon the finished work of Jesus Christ on our behalf, we become a child of God (John 1:12; 2 Corinthians 5:21).

Prayer

I offer You O Lord, my soul, my body, my intellect and my will for I offer You all that I am and have all that I do and say.

I offer You O Lord, all my joys, my sorrows of today, my work with its fatigue, my cross with its bitterness.

I offer You O Lord all those whom I love, those who do me good, who have done me good and those who have recommended themselves to my prayer Amen.

But there are times of greater surrender during a Christian's life, which bring deeper intimacy with God and greater power in service. The more areas of our lives we surrender to Him, the more room there is for the filling of the Holy Spirit (Ephesians 5:18). When we are filled with the Holy Spirit, we exhibit traits of His character (Galatians 5:22). The more we surrender to God, the more our old self-worshiping nature is replaced with one that resembles Christ (2 Corinthians 5:17). While the first time we make a surrender of our life, thoughts, feelings and heart to Holy Spirit is indeed the most powerful, it is useful and helpful to repeat this act of surrender many times per day.

Our Lord is a wise and beneficent victor; He conquers us to bless us. Do we fancy that we are wiser than He? Or that our love for ourselves is more tender and strong than His? Or that we know ourselves better than He does? How our distrust must grieve and wound afresh the tender heart of Him who was for us the Man of Sorrows!

What would be the feelings of an earthly bridegroom if he discovered that his bride-elect was dreading to marry him, lest, when he had the power, he should render her life insupportable? Yet how many of the Lord's redeemed ones treat Him just so! No wonder they are neither happy nor satisfied!

PRAYER IN SILENCE

AND SOLITUDE

St Paul, after his encounter with the risen Christ, spent three days in solitude and silence for prayer and fasting (Acts 9:9). Then after being ministered to by Ananias and visiting with the disciples he withdrew to converse with Christ for three years in the isolation of the Arabian desert (Galatians 1:15-16).

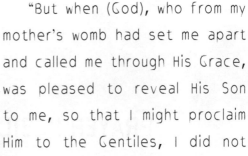

"But when (God), who from my mother's womb had set me apart and called me through His Grace, was pleased to reveal His Son to me, so that I might proclaim Him to the Gentiles, I did not immediately consult flesh and blood, nor did I go up to Jerusalem to those who were apostles before me; rather, I went into Arabia, and then returned to Damascus. Then after three years I went up to Jerusalem," (Galatians 1:17-18).

Apparently St Paul spent three years mostly in solitude and silence in the Arabian desert with the resurrected Christ before he began his ministry. (The other Apostles were with Jesus physically for three years, but for St Paul, like us, he was with Jesus in Spirit for his discipleship and training).

Why Arabia?   It was a time of solitary meditation, in preparation for the Gentile mission. It is probable, he employed himself in studying the Jewish Scriptures more carefully than ever, by the help of the new light which had been bestowed on him; in searching into the true nature of the Law of Moses, and in attending to such revelations as Christ was pleased to make to him. St Paul experienced times of profound revelation from God. Probably this came in solitude, at least in some instances. "The mystery made known to me by revelation, as I have already written briefly," (Ephesians 3:2). "I know a man who was caught up in the third heaven" (2 Corinthians 12:2).

And, by these revelations, he acquired a complete knowledge of all Christ's doctrines, sayings, miracles, sufferings, resurrection, and ascension, and of the design both of the Law and of the Gospel, and of the confirmation which the Gospel derives from the writings of Moses and the prophets. St Paul is saying: I did not learn my Gospel from other human beings, but from the one true God, through the revelation of his son (Galatians 1:13-17).

From Arabia he returned again unto Damascus—where he boldly declared the necessity of believing in Christ, in order to receive salvation, even in the presence of those

Jews whom he knew to be strongly prejudiced against that important doctrine. In the meantime, he increased in strength, as is mentioned in Acts 9:22, confounding the Jews, and proving Jesus to be the very Christ.

Solitude is the creation of an open, empty space in our lives by purposely abstaining from interaction with other human beings, so that, freed from competing loyalties, we can be found by God. Solitude is for being alone with God. It is completed by silence. Solitude and silence is an opportunity to focus on your Intimacy with Jesus, to unhook from your daily responsibilities and the people you interact with, in order to attend to the Lord alone.

The normal way to practice solitude and silence is get alone with God to be quiet in a quiet place for some hours or days. Perhaps you take a walk on a nature trail or sit beside a lake or a creek. Or a quiet spot in a park or your backyard may work well. Even a secluded chair inside your house may work — as long as all your communication and media devices are turned off! The point of your time in solitude and silence is to do nothing and don't try to make anything happen. Do nothing. Don't try to make anything happen.

In solitude and silence you're learning to stop doing, stop producing, stop pleasing people, stop entertaining yourself, stop obsessing — stop doing anything except to simply be your naked self before God and be found by Him.

Fortunately, we don't need to become monks living in private huts in the desert to practice the disciplines of solitude and silence! We can apply the way of the Desert Fathers in the context of the lives we're living. The obvious way to do this is in daily devotions in the Scriptures.

Less obvious is to find quiet interludes during the day to focus our minds on God. A great way to do this is to devote five minutes or more to using a beloved phrase from the Bible in Abiding Prayer. Most people spend time alone driving in the car to work or running errands and this is a great opportunity for solitude and silence if you turn off the radio, CD player, and iPod in order to converse with God.

There are hundreds of Abiding Prayers: They are all simple, compelling phrases (or paraphrases) from the Psalms and other places in the Bible. A favourite Abiding Prayer is "Jesus, be the centre." This little prayer of the heart is based on Mt17:6-8, "The disciples saw Jesus, only Jesus," and Mt21:9, "Jesus was in the centre." It's a simple little prayer that says it all! You might try gently repeating this prayer to yourself now: "Jesus, be the centre..."

It's helpful to use an Abiding Prayer to do some soul work in which we open ourselves to God in order to be formed more into the image of Christ. "Watch and pray," Jesus taught us. We're seeking for Jesus to be our focus and our desire in the activities of the day ahead. Consider your schedule and pray: "As I _____, Jesus, be the centre." that I've used to get settled and centred in Christ.

Submit to God. Jesus prayed on the cross: "Father... into your hands I commit my spirit" (Psalm 31:5; Luke 23:46). This is another powerful, little prayer for our spiritual formation. Try offering this prayer to submit the parts of yourself and your life to God: "Father, into your hands I commit my _____..." (e.g., thoughts; desires; health; relationships; dreams).

Remember we can also abide in prayer for others. Intercede for people the Lord brings to your mind: "Father, into your hands I commit __(name)__"

The ultimate test of the value of solitude and silence is if they empower us to love others: if we've truly been with the God of love and His love is purifying us and putting us at peace then we'll love others better. So we need to realise that silence isn't something only for when we're alone; it's also about learning to control our tongue in our relationships.

In solitude and silence we go into training with Jesus so that we can bring Him, and His wisdom and Grace, into our relationships with others.

"A servant of the Lord is he who in body stands before men. But in mind knocks at heaven in prayer."

– Saint John Climacus

When we're deeply in love with someone we think about them when we get up in the morning and when we go to sleep at night — we think of them all the time!

Spend extended time with Jesus in solitude and silence and you will grow more and more in love with Him!

PRAYER OF INTERCESSION

Upon meeting Jesus face to face on the road to Damascus, St Paul straightaway journeyed into Arabia to meditate on the Scriptures (Galatians 1:17-18). Returning from Arabia, he stepped across the threshold of the synagogue in Damascus to preach Christ crucified and risen. Most of the Jews rejected Christ as Messiah and Saviour. St Paul had deep concern for his people, and he was convinced that without Christ, they were headed for destruction, despite all their advantages. He lists some advantages: "To them belong the adoption as sons, the glory, the covenants, the giving of the Law, the temple worship, and the promises," (Romans 9:4).

It would be helpful to review Israel's condition as revealed in Scripture and with our knowledge from history. The Jews were not in good standing with Rome. During the time of our Lord and the apostles, we know that Israel was under the rule of Rome. Rome governed the land of Palestine by dividing it into various political regions and placing Jewish and Roman officials over the people. Some of the Jews were eager to throw off Roman rule. While the rest might not be willing to resort to violence to gain their freedom, they would welcome it. Many of the Jews refused to admit they were a subject people (John 8:33).

As time went on, Rome seemed to become more and more exasperated with the Jews. In Acts 18:2, Luke records that Claudius commanded all the Jews to leave Rome. It will be only a few years before Rome will have had enough and utterly devastate Jerusalem, killing thousands of the Jews and scattering the rest. Politically speaking, the days of the Jews and of Jerusalem are numbered.

But all of this is more than just a matter of political unrest. It is a part of the divine plan of God. It will be the result of Israel's sin, and specifically of her rejection of Jesus as the Messiah. Jesus was the promised Messiah who had come to save His people and to reign on the throne of David (Luke 1:32-33, 46-55, 68-75). His own people rejected Him, however, and finally crucified Him with the help of Rome. During His earthly life, Jesus warned Israel of the judgment which lay ahead for them (Luke 21:20-24).

The clock was running for Israel and little time was left. In a very few years (less than ten), Rome was to destroy the city of Jerusalem, and the nation which said, "His blood be on us and on our children" (Matthew 27:25) was about to be judged. Israel had failed. They had failed under the old covenant, and they had rejected the new covenant.

"Brethren, my heart's desire and prayer to God for Israel is that they may be saved. For I bear them witness that they have a zeal for God, but not according to knowledge. For they being ignorant of God's righteousness, and seeking to establish their own righteousness, have not submitted to the righteousness of God. For Christ is the end of the Law for righteousness to everyone who believes," (Romans 10:1-4).

St Paul loved the Jews even though they hated him and caused him all sorts of trouble "From the Jews five times I received forty stripes minus one. Three times I was beaten with rods; once I was stoned; ... in perils of my own countrymen," (2 Corinthians 11:24-26). In Romans 10:1, St Paul expresses his hope that the Jews would accept the Gospel: "Brothers and sisters, my heart's desire and prayer to God for Israel is, that they might be saved,". St Paul, the God-appointed apostle to the Gentiles, has his heart set on the salvation of his fellow Jews. He wishes nothing but good for Israel.

"I tell the truth in Christ, I am not lying, my conscience also bearing me witness in the Holy Spirit, that I have great sorrow and continual grief in my heart," (Romans 9:1-2).

"For God is my witness, whom I serve with my spirit in the Gospel of His Son, that without ceasing I make mention of you always in my prayers," (Romans 1:9)

St Paul would like the Jews to encounter the Lord as he did and to experience the beauty and excellence of first love to the Lord. When we intercede in prayer for others we normally describe their needs and make specific petitions to God on their behalf, often going into great detail. Of course, this is a good way to pray.

Another way to intercede for someone is to use a verse or phrase of Scripture to abide in prayer for them. Praying Scripture for others helps us to form effective prayers and to stay focused. And it's a delightful, peaceful, and powerful way of participating in intercessory prayer. Using the words of Scripture to help us intercede, reminds us that prayer is always initiated by God; when we pray we are joining in with the prayers of Christ at the right hand of God and the prayers of the Holy Spirit from deep within us.

To abide in prayer for someone else is to hold him or her in God's presence with you, praying for him or her to be as the branch abiding in the Christ-vine, tended by our loving Father, and bearing fruit by the power of the Holy Spirit.

PRAYER IN THE HOLY SPIRIT

"Likewise the Spirit also helps in our weaknesses. For we do not know what to pray for as we ought, but the Spirit makes intercession for us with groaning which cannot be uttered. Now He who searches the hearts knows what the mind of the Spirit is, because He makes intercession for the saints according to the will of God," (Romans 8:26-27).

In Romans 8:26-27, the Apostle Paul addresses the subject of the assistance of the Holy Spirit to us in our struggles even in moments of simple weaknesses. He intends to arouse our hope and our perseverance as we struggle patiently as He underlines a principal role of the Holy Spirit in our lives. The Spirit offers assistance not only in prayers made on behalf of others, but also assists the person himself. St Paul prayed and asked to see Rome; and Moses prayed as he yearned to see Palestine (Deuteronomy 3:26); Jeremiah prayed on behalf of the Jews (Jeremiah 15:1); and Abraham interceded for the people of Sodom (Genesis 18:23).

Fr Isaak, the disciple of St Anthony: Sometimes we pray for matters that oppose our salvation. Through His divine care, He rejects our requests, for He sees far more than we do what is truly beneficial for us. When St Paul prayed that God would remove the thorn and messenger of Satan which He had allowed for his own benefit: "For this thing I besought the Lord thrice that it might depart from me. And he said unto me, 'My grace is sufficient for thee: for my strength is made perfect in weakness'," (2 Corinthians 12:8, 9).

The Holy Spirit of God Himself who, as the word here used signifies, "helps together", with hope and patience, graces which He has implanted, and which He invigorates and draws forth into act and exercise. The Holy Spirit "helps together" with the saints labouring under their burdens. He also "helps together" with the Father and the Son, who also are helpers of the saints.

St Augustine comments on the Holy Spirit who groans within us as follows: The Holy Spirit does not groan in and within Himself in the Holy Trinity and in His eternal essence...but He groans in us- that is, he makes us groan. That the Holy Spirit makes us groan is not to be considered a simple matter, for He brings us to the realisation that we are strangers living in the land of our estrangement. Moreover, He teaches us to look forward to our homeland and therefore we groan as we greatly yearn for it.

The amazing thing about knowing this promise is that we can rest assured of our future with God. He left nothing up to chance but has done everything to bring restoration to us through His Son Jesus. Today I am so blessed to be called a child of God. I am so blessed to have the Holy Spirit inside of me to testify to this wonderful truth every moment of the day. I pray that this truth blessed you today, Amen!

Dwell upon this truth, beloved. Press it in faith and gladness to your sighing, groaning heart. Is God's hand uplifted? Oh, don't tremble! It is a Father's hand. Don't say that it presses heavily upon you; it is the pressure of love. Oh, don't think that there is one throb of affection less towards you in His heart.

"Likewise the Spirit also helps in our weaknesses. For we do not know what we should pray for as we ought, but the Spirit Himself makes intercession for us with groaning which cannot be uttered. Now He who searches the hearts knows what the mind of the Spirit is, because He makes intercession for the saints according to the will of God," (Romans 8:26-27).

Now St Paul says, "likewise" – in the same way – the Holy Spirit helps us in our weakness. In Romans 8:18-25 St Paul is helping the groaning saints by holding out hope to them as they wait for the redemption of their bodies. Then in verse 26 he says, "Likewise the Spirit helps us in our weakness." I have been helping you in your weakness with the promises of a great future. Romans 8:26-27 answers three questions:

1. What does the Holy Spirit pray for us?

2. How does the Holy Spirit pray for us?

3. Why does the Holy Spirit pray for us?

What Does the Holy Spirit Pray for Us?

First of all, the way that the Spirit helps us in our weakness, namely, by praying for us. Now what does the Spirit ask for when He intercedes for us? The Spirit asks for things that we don't know we should ask for: "We do not know how to pray for what we ought." The Spirit asks for things that we don't know to ask for because of our weakness: "The Spirit helps us in our weakness,"(Romans 8:26). What weakness? Now the word "weakness" in the New Testament can be weakness owing to our limited human nature (Romans 6:19), or weakness owing to sickness (Luke 5:15) or weakness owing to adversity (2 Corinthians 12:9-10).

We certainly know we are to pray for holiness and faith and hope and joy and all the fruits of the Spirit and every other unqualified commandment in the Bible. There is absolutely no doubt that we are to pray for whatever God commands us to do. The revealed will of God is not in question. If God has plainly told us in the Bible to pursue something – like love or faith or righteousness or holiness or courage – then we know we are to pray for it. But this text says that the Spirit is helping us by praying for St Paul says, "Likewise, the Spirit helps us in our weakness." The uncertainty about what we are to pray is because of our "weakness."

So, what is it that we don't know what to pray for in this weakness? The Spirit asks for things that are in accord with the will of God: "The Spirit intercedes for the saints according to the will of God," (Romans 8:27). We don't know the secret will of God about our sicknesses and our hardships! We don't know whether we should pray for healing or for strength to endure. Of course, both are right and it's not wrong to pray for either. But we long to pray with great faith, and we groan that we are not sure what God's way will be with this sickness or this loss or this imprisonment.

We can see some examples of this in St Paul's life. Consider his thorn in the flesh in 2 Corinthians 12. He asked three times that it be removed. And finally Our Lord Jesus revealed to him that His will was not to take it away. Surely, that experience would leave St Paul wondering with every sickness and pain and hardship and imprisonment what God's will was: Healing or not? Deliverance or not? And when he was in prison in Rome he seemed – at least for a time– to be unsure what to pray for – life and ministry, or death with courage. He said, "For to me, to live is Christ, and to die is gain. But if I live on in the flesh, this will mean fruit from my labour; yet what I shall choose I cannot tell. For I am hard-pressed between the two, having a desire to depart and be with Christ, which is far better. Nevertheless, to remain in the flesh is more needful for you," (Philippians 1:22-24).

Now this is painfully relevant to many in the Church now. And it will become increasingly relevant as the price, of being a Christian and a missionary, increases in the years to come. Not only are there many who are sick, but there are some now and there will be many over the next years who are in danger somewhere in the world, and wonder,

"How should we pray?   Should we pray for a safe escape?

Or should we resolve to stay and pray for protection? Or should we stay and pray for courage to suffer and even die?" Our Lord Jesus warned us, "You will be betrayed even by parents and brothers, relatives and friends; and they will put some of you to death. And you will be hated by all for My name's sake. But not a hair of your head shall be lost. By your patience possess your souls," (Luke 21:16-

19). God calls us to take risks. But which risks? When do we risk our lives and the lives of our families and when do we not?

What does the Holy Spirit pray for us?

What the Spirit prays for us is that God would bring about the decisions and circumstances that would most magnify Christ in our lives when we are at a loss as to what the specific will of God is because of our weakness. The "weakness" of verse 26 is the same as the sufferings and decay and futility and groaning of verses 18-25. So this is what the Holy Spirit asks the Father for, but He knows the will of the Father and He asks that the particular decisions and circumstances come to pass which will in fact magnify Christ best.

St Paul's point is that when you groan with Christ-exalting desires but uncertain how Christ might best be magnified, the Spirit prays for you and brings it to pass.

How does the Holy Spirit pray for us?

We are weak and sinful, and St Paul helps us understand how God is for us even in those moments. The Spirit prays for us, in that He moves powerfully in our hearts to create groaning – His groaning experienced as our groaning The Father searches our heart and He hears this groaning. He hears the Christ-exalting yearning in it, and He hears the Spirit's clear intention that certain decisions and circumstances come about in the exact way that will bring the most glory to Our Lord Jesus.

Why does the Holy Spirit pray for us?

God created the universe and all that is in it to display the riches of the glory of His Grace. To know more of God's purpose will deepen our commitment to pray and help us glorify God for why He does what He does. Prayer for God's help is one way that God preserves and manifests the dependence of His people on His Grace and power. The necessity of prayer is a constant reminder and display of our dependence on God for everything, so that He gets the glory when we get the help. "Call upon me in the day of trouble; I will deliver you, and you shall glorify me," (Psalm 50:15). "Whatever you ask in My Name, this I will do, that the Father may be glorified in the Son," (John 14:13).

 When you feel very weak, because of suffering or decay or sickness or futility or persecution or failed plans or baffling decisions, don't despair, as if God is angry with you or at your inability to know what to do or what to pray. At that very moment, experience the wordless groanings of your heart as groanings for the glory of Christ. And trust the Spirit of God to intercede for you about the specifics. Trust Him, that because He is praying for you, your Father will bring about decisions and circumstances that will magnify Christ in the best way — in the very midst of your ignorance and groaning.

What a gracious and merciful God we have! He has planned for all our weakness and nothing can separate us from His love! What a view do these two verses (Romans 8:26-27) give of the relations subsisting between the Divine Persons in the economy of redemption, and the harmony of their respective operations in the case of each of the redeemed!

PRAYER OF THANKSGIVING

"First, I thank my God through Our Lord Jesus Christ for you all, that your faith is spoken of (rather, proclaimed) in the whole world," Rom1:8. The importance and spiritual benefits of thanksgiving in our prayer life cannot be over-emphasised. The Bible tells us God resists the proud but gives grace to the humble (James 4:6). But the question is: how do you become humble? It is done by being thankful.

A good rule is to be worried for nothing (Philippians 4:6); be prayerful in all things (1 Thessalonians 5:18), and be thankful for anything. It was the sin of thanklessness that caused the ancient world to plunge into the terrible depths of sexual depravity (Romans 1:21). In the Old Testament, a special group of priests was appointed to do nothing else but pray and thank the Lord (2 Chronicles 31:2).

The object of thanksgiving is God not merely as a creator and preserver, but as a Father, the Father of Christ, and our Father in Christ; as the one God, and our God, Father, Son, and Spirit. The apostle styles Him, my God; which distinguishes Him from all others. No pagan would have made such a statement, nor would have most Jews referred to God with the personal pronoun 'my'. "My God" also points out his particular interest in Him, expresses his knowledge of Him and faith in Him, and demonstrates that what he did now, he did in faith. For St Paul, his personal relationship with God was not a theological abstraction but an intimate acquaintance with his beloved Saviour and Friend.

 Is He your God, your best Friend? There can be no other and none better. Beloved, if He is "your" God, then remember that "you have not received a spirit of slavery leading to fear again, but you have received a spirit of adoption as sons by which we cry out, "Abba Father!" (Romans 8:15, Galatians 4:6, Mark 14:36). In these passages, Abba is the Aramaic term for "Father" conveying a picture of intimacy, much like our English words "Daddy" or "Papa", the overall picture being one of tenderness, dependence, and a relationship free of fear or anxiety.

'First' means first in time, place, order, importance. 'Thank' is in the present tense which denotes that St Paul's continual gratitude to God, the Giver of good thing bestowed and every perfect gift (James 1:17). The first mark of true spiritual service, which St Paul had in abundance, is thankfulness. It is also the mark of a Spirit filled (controlled) man (Ephesians 5:20; Colossians 3:16-17). St Paul was grateful for what God had done for and through him, but he was equally grateful for what God had done in and through other believers.

A continual attitude of gratitude can make a sour day sweet. Do you give God this kind of quality time, offering thanks to Him? Do you thank Him first or last (or not at all)? Make Him your priority when you rise, when you walk about and when you lie down to sleep (Proverbs 6:20-22). Make thanksgiving to your worthy God first on your "day timer"! You won't regret it.

A thankful heart for those to whom one ministers is essential to true spiritual service. The Christian who is trying to serve God's people, however needy they may be, without gratitude in his heart for what the Lord has done for them will find his service lacking joy. St Paul could usually find a cause for thanks so that he could honour the Lord for what had been done already and hope for what God would use him to do. Superficial believers are seldom satisfied and therefore seldom thankful. Because they focus on their own appetites for things of the world, they are more often resentful than thankful. A thankless heart is a selfish, self-centred, legalistic heart. St Paul had a thankful heart because he continually focused on what God was doing in his own life, in the lives of other faithful believers, and in the advancement of His kingdom throughout the world.

Through Our Lord Jesus Christ: The person through whom thanks are given is Our Lord Jesus Christ. He is the believer's Great High Priest, through Whom we have confidence access to the throne of God the Father (Hebrews 2:17-18, 4:14-16, 10:19-22). This phrase pictures Our Lord Jesus as our Mediator, "There is one God and one Mediator also between God and men, the man Christ Our Lord Jesus (1Timothy 2:5). There is no coming to God but through Christ, nor is any sacrifice either of prayer or praise acceptable without Him, and since all we have come through Him, it is but reasonable that thanks for them should be returned by and through Him.

Through Him (Christ) then, let us continually offer up a sacrifice of praise to God, that is, the fruit of lips that give thanks to His name. "You also, as living stones, are being built up as a spiritual house for a holy priesthood, to offer up spiritual sacrifices acceptable to God through Jesus Christ.,"(1 Peter 2:5). "I am the way, and the truth, and the life; no one comes to the Father, but through Me," (John 14:6). All things are from Him, through Him and to Him. To Him be the glory forever. Amen.

The Holy Scriptures: Love Holy Scriptures and wisdom will love you. Love her, and she will keep you. Honour her, and she will embrace you.

— St Jerome

STRIVING IN PRAYER

"Now I beg you, brethren, through the Lord Jesus Christ, and through the love of the Spirit, that you strive together with me in prayers to God for me, that I may be delivered from those in Judea who do not believe, and that my service for Jerusalem may be acceptable to the saints, that I may come to you with joy by the will of God, and may be refreshed together with you. Now the God of peace be with you all. Amen," (Romans 15:30-32).

St Paul was confident that after he had delivered this offering, that Christ would bless his mission to Rome and Spain. He asks them to help him in his difficult mission by praying for him. As Acts 21 confirms, the most dangerous part of the trip was not the voyage, but the disobedient Jews (an ironic contrast to the obedient Gentiles). St Paul did not assume that the believers would be glad to see him, either — he wanted prayer that they might accept the offering he was bringing. Some did not want to accept the fact that Gentiles were now in the family of faith.

Incentives to Strive in Prayer

"Now I beg you, brethren, through the Lord Jesus Christ, and through the love of the Spirit, that you strive together with me in prayers to God for me," (Romans 15:30). The basic point of the verse is to motivate the Roman Christians to "strive" or to "struggle" or to "fight" in prayer to God for St Paul as he goes to Jerusalem with a contribution for the poor Christians of the city. It is a plea not for casual, laid back, easy-going prayer, but for striving or struggling in prayer. Then there are two incentives for them to respond to this plea. He pleads "by the Lord Jesus Christ" and he pleads "by the love of the Spirit".

God's customary way to move your will is through your mind. That is, He typically draws the will into action by displaying truth to the mind. So in this case, through St Paul, God desires that the will of the Roman Christians incline to pray — and not just incline but incline vigorously. He calls it "striving" in prayer. So to awaken their will to this kind of vigorous inclination, and pull it out into dynamic action, he puts two God-cantered truths in their minds:

- Jesus Christ is Lord ("by our Lord Jesus Christ"); and

- The Holy Spirit is a Spirit of love ("by the love of the Spirit").

Since Jesus is Lord, you may pray with confidence that He has the right and authority and power to restrain the disobedient in Judea. And since the Spirit of God is a Spirit of love, you can pray with confidence that He will lovingly fill the saints in Jerusalem with love for St Paul so that his ministry is accepted and not resented. So, the energetic vigorous responses of the heart in prayer (and other ways) are meant by God to be responses to great God-centred truth — in this case, Jesus is Lord of the universe; and the Spirit is full of love. Why is this? Why is it not God's usual way to just tell us to do things without giving us incentives like this to do them?

God would not get glory for our actions if they were not stimulated by views of God. God is in the main business in the world of magnifying the worth of His Son and the power of His Spirit and the glory of His Own Name. So His will is that we be aware of these things. That we know them. That we think on them, and that they become conscious incentives in the way we make choices and the way we get stirred up to pray.

"Now I beg you, brethren, through the Lord Jesus Christ, and through the love of the Spirit, that you strive together with me in prayers to God for me," (Romans 15:30). St Paul says, he is praying for the same thing. So if he is praying, why does he need more people praying? The divine purpose of prayer is to magnify the greatness of God. Prayer exists for the glory of God. Jesus said, "And whatever you ask in my name, that will I do, that the Father may be glorified in the Son," (John 14:13). The aim of prayer is that the Father be glorified through Jesus. So the more people there are praying for something, and thus depending on God for mercy and power, the more people will give Him thanks and glorify Him when the answer comes. Prayer changes people's wills. Or, more accurately, God changes people's wills in answer to prayer.

St Paul's two prayer requests are:

• "That I may be delivered from those who are disobedient in Judea", and

• "that my service for Jerusalem may prove acceptable to the saints."

So he had two concerns:

- That the non-Christians in Judea would kill him and end his ministry; and

- That the Christians would find fault with his ministry.

So St Paul urges the Roman Christians a few thousand Km from Jerusalem to ask God not to let that happen. The implication is that the will of the unbelievers to hurt St Paul and the will of the believers to disapprove St Paul's ministry are both in the power of God to change. There would seem to be no point in praying for these two things if God could not do them. In both cases the wills of people are involved and the answer to the prayer is going to involve God changing those wills — in the one case so that the ill-will of unbelievers is restrained, and in the other case so that the good will of believers is assured.

 *Since Jesus is Lord, you may pray with confidence that He has the right and authority and power to restrain the disobedient in Judea. And since the Spirit of God is a Spirit of love, you can pray with confidence that He will lovingly fill the saints*

in Jerusalem with love for St Paul so that his
ministry is accepted and not resented.

PRAYER OF PRAISE

We are created to praise and glorify the Lord day by
day. Our life should be a song of praise to the glory of God.
Is praising God a selfish desire on God's part? Certainly
not. Praise was the purpose for which He created us. We
ought to voluntarily give praise daily.

 Where the heart belongs:
our hearts are made for you,
O Lord, and they are restless
until they rest in you.

— St Augustine

Praise is to bestow approval upon; to honour; to
worship; to glorify; commendation. The Hebrew word
"yadah" means "to stretch out the hand", and is translated
"praise". That is, to hold out the hands in reverence, to
open the hands and let go of everything, just stand and
praise God open-handedly.

Our problem is to let go of things, to let go of our problems and service and give ourselves to praising the Lord. We only praise something that we honour and prize highly. If we hold the Lord in the highest state of respect and admiration it will be easy to praise Him.

We should praise the Lord in sickness, in adversity and in health and prosperity. We should praise the Lord for anything and everything (Philippians 4:6). The true Christian is one who can trust and praise the Lord even through blinding tears. It is enough to know that God plans and does all things well (Romans 8:28).

Perhaps we realise that we have not praised enough. Pray that God will teach us to praise Him much more in the future, beginning today. "O Lord, open Thou my lips (Psalm 51:15). Cause me to praise You more and more."

Praise is the precious privilege of every Christian believer in Jesus Christ. Sing a great deal. This is one good way to praise the Lord. If people praise us for our accomplishments, let us be sure to pass the praise to Him. It is easy to praise one who is truly worthy of praise, and Jesus is worthy (Revelations 5:9). It is easier for His children to give God money or service than praise. Praise is an attitude of the heart (1 Colossians 10:31), whatsoever we do, we should do for His glory.

Remember God more than you breathe.

– St Gregory Nazianzen

What is the most important thing in life? Is it to earn a living? To be saved and go to heaven? To serve God? I believe the answer is to praise God. Man's chief end is to glorify God and to enjoy Him forever. "Even every one that is called by My name: for I have created him for My glory," (Isaiah 43:7).

Doxology to God's Ways

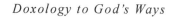

"Oh, the depth of the riches both of the wisdom and knowledge of God! How unsearchable are His judgments and His ways past finding out! 'For who has known the mind of the Lord? Or who has become His counsellor?' 'Or who has first given to Him and it shall be repaid to him?' For of Him and through Him and to Him are all things, to whom be glory forever. Amen," (Romans 11:33-36, Isaiah 40:13, Job 41:11).

"O the depth of the riches both of the wisdom and knowledge of God! how unsearchable are His judgments, and His ways past finding out!" (Romans 11:33). So we would never have arrived at this knowledge of God without divine revelation. The "riches" spoken of, "the wisdom and knowledge of God" are comprehended in the cross of Christ, which is the sacrifice for the sinners of this world. Again, there is an overwhelming sense that God's "ways" of reaching humanity are beyond human devising. Indeed, it is God's work and He is the one who will finish it.

So St Paul launches into a section of praise. It is a call to theological and intellectual humility — and it is also a reminder that theology, if done correctly, should always lead us to praise and worship. Whenever we catch a glimpse of what God has done or is doing, we should respond with awe and thanksgiving. St Paul ends by praising the God who can be counted on to succeed: "For of Him and through Him and to Him are all things. To Him be glory forever! Amen,"(Romans 11:36).

The apostle Paul knew the Mysteries of the Kingdom of God as well as ever any man; yet he confesses himself at a loss; and despairing to find the bottom, he humbly sits down at the brink, and adores the depth. Those who know most in this imperfect state, feel their own weakness most. There is not only depth in the Divine counsels, but riches; abundance of that which is precious and valuable. The Divine counsels are complete; they have not only depth and height, but breadth and length (Ephesians 3:18) and that passing knowledge.

The apostle Paul is overwhelmed at the depth of the riches both of the wisdom and the knowledge of God; and here is where we all join St Paul in adoring contemplation of God's counsels, the wisdom with which He brings them forth, and the knowledge of man and of his heart and his history, past, present, and future, that He displays in it all. There is that vast distance and disproportion between God and man, between the Creator and the creature, which for ever shuts us from knowledge of His ways. What man shall teach God how to govern the world?

The apostle adores the sovereignty of the Divine counsels. All things in heaven and earth, especially those which relate to our salvation, that belong to our peace, are all of Him by way of creation, through Him by way of providence, that they may be to Him in their end: Of God, as the Spring and Fountain of all; through Christ, to God, as the end. These include all God's relations to His creatures; if all are of Him, and through Him, all should be to Him, and for Him. Whatever begins, let God's glory be the end: especially let us adore Him when we talk of the Divine counsels and acting. The saints in heaven never dispute, but always praise.

 When I think about what God has done in my life, do I respond with praise (verses 33–36)? What would I include in my poem of praise? Praise God, who in His Grace saves all peoples! He is faithful to His promises, and His purpose will stand.

Now may God give us Grace to realise at least a little of our mighty privilege in having revealed to us the mind of the Lord, the God of hosts "as it has now been revealed by the Spirit to His holy apostles and prophets: that the

Gentiles should be fellow heirs, of the same body, and partakers of His promise through the Gospel," (Ephesians 3:5-6). God has today "made us alive together with Christ, and raised us up with Him, and made us sit in the heavenly places in Christ Jesus," (Ephesians 2:6). "For me to live is Christ!" (Philippians 1:21). We are in Christ, and Christ is in us, "the hope of glory!"

The Holy Scriptures... they are not simply words, but words of the Holy Spirit, and hence the treasure to be found in even a single syllable is great. ... we are listening to God speaking to us through the tongue of the inspired authors.

— St John Chrysostom

St Paul includes a brief prayer: "Now may the God of patience and comfort grant you to be like-minded toward one another, according to Christ Jesus, that you may with one mind and one mouth glorify the God and Father of our Lord Jesus Christ," (Romans 15:5-6). That is, may God give you the attitude of service that leads to worship together. To bridge distinctions of worship, St

Paul focused on building unity through following Our Lord
Jesus Christ (verse 5). In unity Christians glorify God and
Our Lord Jesus (verse 6). Christians accept a life of service
and sacrifice, even when it is not comfortable to do so.
Freedom in Our Lord Jesus means leaving comfort zones
to bear with those who do not share the same approach
to liberty.

 Imitate the sacrifice of Our
Lord Jesus Christ (Romans
15:1-6). Our Lord Jesus did not
become a human sacrifice for us
because it was the comfortable
thing to do. He came to serve, to save and to
be sacrificed.

Just as Our Lord Jesus gave up His privileges to serve
us, we should be willing to give up some of ours, so people
will praise God. Reconciliation with God should lead us
toward reconciliation with other people.

"Or who has first given to Him that it might be paid
back to him again? For from Him and through Him and
to Him are all things. To Him be the glory forever. Amen,"
Rom11:35-36. Is it not interesting that we Christians are

eager to get to the application? I fear that often this is because we are self-centred. Application focuses on us — we think. If we think this, we are wrong! St Paul's application focuses our attention on God and our praise toward God. That is where it belongs. That is where our focus always belongs. That is where our focus eternally will be. That is where our focus should be now.

A servant of the Lord is he who in body stands before men. But in mind knocks at heaven in prayer.

— St John Climacus

It is that which should warm our hearts now and turn our hearts toward God, where we find salvation, peace, joy, hope, love, and all that is worthy of praise.

It is not our convictions which should consume us. Nor should it be the differences we have with our fellow-believers. It is God who should consume us. May we be caught up — lost in Him — in His glory, honour, wisdom, and power. Let us join St Paul and all of the saints of all the ages, in praising God. To God be the glory, great things

He has done!

"Now may the God of hope fill you with all joy and peace in believing, that you may abound in hope by the power of the Holy Spirit," (Romans 15:13).

PRAY WITHOUT CEASING -

THE JESUS PRAYER

We are all called to "pray without ceasing", says St Paul in (1 Thessalonians 5:17). The real questions is, how. The "Jesus Prayer" provides one good way to pray constantly. In fact, the Jesus Prayer is the most widespread and most specifically Orthodox spiritual prayer. Our task is to draw nearer to God.

It is impossible to draw near to God by any means other than increasing prayer.

– St Isaac of Syria

The classical form of the Jesus Prayer is, "Lord Jesus Christ, Son of God, have mercy on me, a sinner." The actual words of our short prayers can vary. We might say the classic version of the Jesus Prayer, or we might say, "Lord Jesus Christ, have mercy on me." We may say, "Lord Jesus, have mercy." Or, we might say a Psalm verse, or a Bible quote, or some other prayer. Monks of old said, "Lord, make haste to help me. Lord, make speed to save me," all day long.

The history of the Jesus Prayer goes back, as far as we know, to the early sixth century; it was taught that repetition of the prayer leads to inner stillness. Even earlier John Cassian recommended this type of prayer. In the fourth century Egypt, in Nitria, short "arrow" prayers were practiced.

There is no need to waste time with words. It is enough to hold out your hands and say, "Lord, according to your desire and your wisdom, have mercy." If pressed in the struggle, say, "Lord, save me!" or say, "Lord". He knows what is best for us, and will have mercy upon us. — Abba Macarius of Egypt

St John Chrysostom tells us how this can happen: 'I implore you, brethren, never to break or to despise the rule of this prayer: A Christian when he eats, drinks, walks, sits, travels or does any other thing must continually cry: 'Lord Jesus Christ, Son of God, have mercy upon me', so that the name of the Lord Jesus descending into the depths of the heart, should subdue the serpent ruling over the inner pastures and bring life and salvation to the soul.

He should always live with the name of the Lord Jesus, so that the heart swallows the Lord and the Lord the heart, and the two become one.

Do not estrange your heart from God, but abide in Him, and always guard your heart by remembering our Lord Jesus Christ, until the name of the Lord becomes rooted in the heart and it ceases to think anything else.' – St John Chrysostom:

'Continue constantly in the name of the Lord Jesus that the heart may swallow the Lord and the Lord the heart, and that these two may be one. However, this is not accomplished in a single day, and not in two days, but requires many years and much time.'

– Orthodox Fathers

What is so different about the Jesus Prayer? Prayer, to the average man, is asking God for something. The Jesus Prayer is not this. It is an attempt - a scientific attempt - to change the one who prays. There is tremendous power in the name of Jesus. St Paul says, "Everyone who calls upon the name of the Lord will be saved," (Roans m10:13). Again, he writes to the Philippians, "Christ Jesus... humbled himself and became obedient to death, even death on a cross. Therefore, God has highly exalted Him and given Him the name that is above every name, that in the name of Jesus every knee should bow, of things in heaven, and things on earth and things under the earth," (Philippians 2:5-10). Jesus says in John 14:13, "If you ask anything in My name, I will do it." St Peter says, "And there is salvation in no one else, for there is no other name under heaven given among men by which we must be saved," (Acts 4:12).

The power of the "Jesus Prayer", then, lies in the name of Jesus, "the name that is above every name". Thus, the name "Jesus" alone can fulfil the need of one who prays when it is prayed with faith and with a life that is lived in obedience to Christ. For, as our Lord said, "Not everyone who says to me 'Lord, Lord', shall enter the kingdom of heaven but he who does the will of My Father who is in heaven,"(Matthew 7:21).

The Jesus prayer can give us the same power to resist every evil thought and temptation with which Satan attacks us. For example, when Satan knocks on the door

'With the name of Jesus flog the foes, because there is no stronger weapon in heaven or earth'.

— St John Climacus

PRAYING WITH ST PAUL

Chosen to Proclaim the Good News

We thank you, Father, (Galatians 1:15) that each of us is your work of art (Ephesians 2:10), chosen specially long ago to live through love in your presence (Ephesians 1:3-4) and be joyful envoys, radiant ambassadors for Christ (2 Corinthians 2:17;5:20), reflecting your brightness like mirrors (2 Corinthians 3:18) in conveying Good News to the people you love (1 Thessalonians 2:4; Romans 1:7).

May your Spirit enable us to shine in the world like bright stars (Philippians 2:16) in offering it the word of life. We proclaim 'Christ among us, our hope of glory' (Colossians 1:27; Acts 28:20), appreciating that Jesus fulfilled the scriptures as well as people's hopes (Acts 28:20; 1 Corinthians 15:3) in all that He said and did.

Free-Given Grace

None of us can 'earn' salvation, Father; nobody can 'earn' your healing and forgiveness. It is by your freely-given grace that we are saved (Romans 11:6), and our good deeds are simply a response to your loving actions. Our relationship with you, Father, is 'made right' through the abundant and free gift of your Grace (Romans 3:24; 5:15) which you shower upon us, redeeming us in Christ (Ephesians 1:7; Romans 3:24).

Reconciled, Justified, At One with You

To be restored, to live 'at one' with you, Father, needed the offering of a perfect sacrifice (Ephesians 5:2). That sacrifice was offered by our brother, Jesus the Lord (1 Timothy 2:5; Romans 5:15-19; Galatians 1:4) whom St Paul also describes as the only Son of God (Acts 9:20; Colossians 2:9). And so in Jesus - fully human and fully God - we are fulfilled and 'justified', Father, (Colossians 2:9; Romans 3:24-26) made right and reconciled with you.

Bought and Paid For

Through the life, death and resurrection of your Son you have dealt with sin and death, Father, (Romans 8:14) taking away the power that they had over us.

To you, Father, each of us must give an account of ourselves (Romans 14:12) and we thank you for giving us the victory (1 Corinthians 15:57) through our Lord, Jesus Christ.

The Cross, after all, is your power to save (1 Corinthians 1:18). You do not hold our sins against us, Father, (2 Corinthians 5:19) and Jesus, by nailing them to the Cross (Galatians 2:19-21) has done away with every record of the debt that we owed (Colossians 2:14).

In a sermon of his, St Paul is the only one to mention that Jesus said: "There is more happiness in giving than in receiving" (Acts2 0:35), and we rejoice that in Jesus, we gain our freedom, the forgiveness of our sins (Colossians 1:14), and we acknowledge that we have been bought and paid for (1 Corinthians 6:20; 7:23).

Encountering Jesus

St Paul declared that nothing can happen (Philippians 3:8-9) that can outweigh the supreme advantage of knowing, of relating to, Christ Jesus our Lord. Christ is our life (Colossians 3:4) and we are called to encounter Him personally.

We join St Paul in proclaiming that all we "want is to know Christ and the power of His resurrection" (Philippians 3:10).

Everyday Life

In our everyday life, Father, we pray for the Spirit to inspire and empower us that we may show forth our faith in action (1 Thessalonians 1:3), beside all the people you love in our world of today.

It is in our everyday lives that we are planted in love and built on love (Ephesians 3:17) to follow Christ by loving as he loved us (Ephesians 5:2), and we ask that your Spirit may enable us, Father, to encourage each other in our common faith (Romans 1:12; 1 Thessalonians 5:11), putting fresh heart into your people (Acts 14:22; Philemon 1:7,20).

We are conscious, too, that your goodness, Father, is meant to lead us to repentance (Romans 2:4).

May our minds be filled with everything that is true

and noble, good and pure (Philippians 4:8), and all that is virtuous and worthy of praise.

We pray that our love may never be a pretence (Romans 12:9) but that we may have a profound respect for each person, (2 Corinthians 1:12; Romans 12:10-13) resisting evil and conquering it with good (Romans 12:21).

May we be kept firm and strong in the faith (1 Thessalonians 3:2).

Jesus Is Lord; Resurrection; We Are Heirs

We proclaim the Good News, Father, that Jesus is Lord (Romans 10:9; Acts 23:6), and that you raised him from death.

He is the first-fruits of all who 'fall asleep' (1 Corinthians 15:20), and so each of us can consider Jesus as our eldest brother: (Romans 8:29) the one to lead us through what He first experienced.

Being heirs to an inheritance reminds us of so much

that really matters, that is precious, of pride in heritage, of treasuring family love and memories, of us belonging to something greater which, at the same time, belongs to us.

And so we are proud to say, Father, that we are your heirs (Romans 8:16-17) called to inherit great riches (2 Corinthians 4:14; Romans 8:34) and have promises fulfilled: for no reason except your own compassion! (Titus 3:5-8).

The Spirit in Us

We rejoice that your love, faithful God (2 Thessalonians 3:3) has been poured into our hearts by the Holy Spirit (Romans 5:5) who has made his home in each of us (Romans 8:9) enabling us to turn to you and pray intimately: (Galatians 4:6-7 "Abba, Father" (Romans 8:15, 26-27).

It is by co-operating with your Spirit, that we can put to good use the various gifts with which you have lovingly graced us (1 Corinthians 7:7; 12:11; 2 Corinthians 6:1).

You lavish us with your riches, Father, (Philippians 4:19; 1 Timothy 6:17) and there is no limit to the blessings you send, (2 Corinthians 9:8) enabling our witness to Christ to be strong. (1 Corinthians 1:6).

There are times, in fact, when the love of Christ overwhelms us (2 Corinthians 5:14), and we remain convinced (Romans 8:28-39) that nothing can ever come between us and your love, Father, made visible in Christ Jesus, our Lord.

Many are the trials through which we triumph (Romans 8:37-39) by the power of him who loved us.

Suffering

Each of us knows, Father, that your power is at its best when our own weakness is evident (2 Corinthians 12:9-10), and we pray that we may retain the lived conviction that to suffer in your way (2 Corinthians 7:10) means changing for the better, and leaves no regrets.

St Paul reminds us that what we suffer in this life (Romans 8:18; 2 Corinthians 4:17) can never be compared to the glory which is waiting for us and adds that, if we have hope - if we truly have conviction (Romans 12:12; Titus 2:13-14) - then that will make us joyful.

In all our sorrows, Father, there can be benefit for other people: you give us inexhaustible comfort (2 Thessalonians 2:16-17) and such sure conviction that we are enabled to bring your own comfort and consolation to others (2 Corinthians 1:4).

Appreciation

We pray that, for each of us, our attitude may always be (Colossians 1:3; 3:16; Ephesians 1:16; Philippians 1:3); that of appreciation and thankfulness (1 Thessalonians 1:2; 5:17; 2 Thessalonians 2:13).

We thank you that you have enriched us in so many ways, especially in those people who have embodied qualities of the Spirit: (Galatians 5:21-22) showing love, joy and peace, patience, kindness and goodness, trustfulness, gentleness and self-control.

Messengers of The Good News

Bless, Father, the people to whom we hand on your Good News (2 Timothy 2:3) that they may have much joy and peace in their faith (Romans 15:13) so that they in turn will be able to proclaim to others that the Good News is 'the power of God saving all who have faith' (Romans 1:16).

Then the message of Christ in all its richness (Colossians 3:16) will find a home, Father, in all those for whom you have created a place (Colossians 1:13) in the Kingdom of your dear Son. Amen.

Behind St Paul's boundless energy as apostle, missionary, pastor and theologian (as well as tentmaker!) must have been an extraordinary prayer life. For St Paul, the line between all of Christian life and prayer is thin or non-existent. St Paul models for us the integration of prayer and life.

There are many ways of praying, and St Paul seems to have experienced and to have referred to the full range. One of the very first prayers that St Paul ever addressed to Christ became his life's quest of faith, obedience, and submission; a quest that we do well to imitate. Prayer in silence and solitude (in Arabia) was St Paul's way of "thirsting for the Lord", and his eagerness to know His will. Prayer is invaluable for growing in the virtues needed to carry God's will out. Much more common are his references to the importance of intercessory prayer, thanksgiving, prayer without ceasing, and praise.

St Paul teaches that prayer involves a great and vital

communion with the Holy Spirit. We pray in confidence knowing that the Holy Spirit is speaking the true prayer of our heart to the Father in a language that only God Himself can comprehend.

St Paul's prayer models have greatly enriched the prayer life of the Church and I pray they enrich yours too.